HELLO PURPOSE
MY FRIEND!

31 Days of Discovering
Your Relationship with Purpose

Coming soon!

CYCLES
STOP THE MADNESS!

Pressured Beauty

HELLO PURPOSE MY FRIEND!

31 Days of Discovering Your Relationship with Purpose

Kerra Slaughter

HELLO PURPOSE MY FRIEND!
31 Days of Discovering Your Relationship with Purpose

Second Edition: March 2017
Printed in the United States of America

ISBN: 978-0-578-20276-1

This book is dedicated to
Quincy Sr., Tay, Belle, Quincy Jr.,
Israel and King Solomon.
To the best Motivational Speaker in my world,
Keri Kokayi

TABLE OF CONTENTS

❀

❀

ACKNOWLEDGMENTS

I would like to first acknowledge my mother and father, Terry and Virginia Whorton.

I would like to also acknowledge my brother and sisters; I love you all!

I would like to also take time to acknowledge the two in my threefold cord, my right hand and my life saver. Thank you so much right hand for all that you do, for collaborating with me to get everything typed up and all the editing completed. Thank you for working day and night to make sure everything was professional. Words can't express how much I really appreciate everything you do. Your prayers and hard work do not go unnoticed.

Next, I would like to acknowledge my editor, Julie Pearson. You are an amazing big sister in Christ. I have learned so much from watching you, from listening to your wise counsel, and from mimicking the love of Christ that resides in you. Thank you for seeing in me what I didn't.

Lastly, I would like to acknowledge my dearest. Dearest cousin, I am blessed to have you. Outside of my husband, you are my biggest supporter from the beginning of ministry. My cheerleader and my protector. I always feel safe from anybody when you are around. Thank you for seeing my purpose before I did.

PREFACE

There is power in seeing purpose as a person. Although you know purpose is the gifting inside you that was given when God designed you, your perception changes when you can see it speaking, whispering, guiding, desiring and becoming your friend.

The quality of who you become is apparent in how you treat every obstacle and trial. Staying focused on your purpose must become your number one priority. When you are focused on purpose, putting God first is priority! Purpose ensures the increase for the love of your family and yourself.

Purpose was never designed for you to hate it or life. So if you are doing something now that you hate, you are not walking in your purpose.

The key to enjoying life and being happy even when you are not having the best day is to perfect your purpose. This is 31 days of enjoying your new found friend called Purpose. This book will encourage you, move you forward and thrust you into your best place that life has to offer you. God designed it that way. Say "hello" to your new life coach called Purpose.

PURPOSE 1

Purpose has an amazing way of showing us what we were made to do.

PONDER

Purpose is given by God. Are you allowing it to direct you? If you see where purpose is taking you; don't fight it, follow it.

PRAYER

God, help me to walk in my divine, God-given purpose by submitting to your will and to follow you. In Jesus name, amen.

"I will instruct thee and teach thee in the way which thou shalt go: I will guide thee with mine eye."
— Psalm 32:8 KJV

WHAT IS PURPOSE TELLING YOU?

_____

_____

_____

_____

_____

_____

_____

_____

_____

_____

_____

_____

_____

_____

PURPOSE 2

Purpose has an instinctive way of showing up with hope; it allows you to see your future.

PONDER

The purpose God has given you is innate, natural and inherent. You were born to do it. Find it!

PRAYER

God, show me what I think about first outside of you in the morning, what I think about most during the day, and what dominates and drives my future at night. Then, I will know my true purpose. In Jesus name, amen.

"For I know the plans I have for you, 'declares the Lord,' plans to prosper you and not to harm you, plans to give you hope and a future."
                                    — Jeremiah 29:11 NIV

WHAT IS PURPOSE TELLING YOU?

_____

_____

_____

_____

_____

_____

_____

_____

_____

_____

_____

_____

_____

_____

PURPOSE 3

Purpose explains to me why what I am doing is not what will satisfy me.

PONDER

If you wake up frustrated with your day, feel defeated and broken by life and feel you are not contributing your best "you" to life; ask yourself: "Am I living and fulfilling my destiny or am I settling for what I already have in my hand?" Remember, what you already have in your hand has the power to fund your purpose.

PRAYER

God, help me to use what you have given me to perfect what is concerning me. My concern is my desire to move in divine alignment with the things of God, for my life. Show me, clearly. In Jesus name, amen.

"The Lord will perfect that which concernth me: thy mercy, O Lord, endureth forever: forsake not the works of thine own hands."

— Psalms 138:8 KJV

WHAT IS PURPOSE TELLING YOU?

_____

_____

_____

_____

_____

_____

_____

_____

_____

_____

_____

_____

_____

PURPOSE 4

Purpose whispers, "You are too great to lose focus!"

PONDER

Distractions are the enemy to purpose. Find your place where you shut out the world, turn off your phone, clear your head and focus your entire self on what God has called you to do. Ask yourself, "Could it be that what I think is helping me, is distracting me?"

PRAYER

Holy Spirit, please give me the power and strength to remove every person, thing and idea that distracts me and knocks me off my focus. Remove these things far from me. In Jesus name, amen.

"Let thine eyes look right on, and let thine eyelids look straight before thee." — Proverbs 4:25 KJV

"And this I speak for your own profit; not that I may cast a snare upon you, but for that which is comely, and that ye may attend upon the Lord without distraction." — 1 Corinthians 7:35 KJV

WHAT IS PURPOSE TELLING YOU?

_____

_____

_____

_____

_____

_____

_____

_____

_____

_____

_____

_____

_____

_____

PURPOSE 5

Purpose is speaking and telling me to, "Stay on the path that's leading me to my meaning."

PONDER

My meaning explains who I am. It's the discovery of my interpretation. Remember, the enemy puts things in place to keep you from understanding YOU! Don't allow the outside to get on the inside and contaminate your meaning.

PRAYER

By the authority of the Holy Spirit, I walk in my true meaning. I know who I am. I know who God designed me to be. I will continually walk in the path that God has laid out for me. In Jesus name, amen.

"For we are his workmanship, created in Christ Jesus unto good works, which God hath before ordained that we should walk in them."
— Ephesians 2:10 KJV

WHAT IS PURPOSE TELLING YOU?

_____

_____

_____

_____

_____

_____

_____

_____

_____

_____

_____

_____

_____

_____

PURPOSE 6

Purpose is directing me to stay clear of chatter. It breaks my focus.

PONDER

Too much talking can cause confusion. When everyone is trying to direct you and no one is listening to you, it subtracts focus from you. Remember, your ears have a filter. You don't need to receive everything. Your feet have wisdom, so walk away when the conversation goes from critiquing you to criticizing you.

PRAYER

Dear Heavenly Father, remove, far from me, mouths that come to hurt me. With the authority given by the Holy Spirit, I close every mouth open to destroy my purpose. In Jesus name, amen.

"Go from the presence of a foolish man, when thou perceives not in him the lips of knowledge."
— Proverbs 14:7 KJV

WHAT IS PURPOSE TELLING YOU?

_____

_____

_____

_____

_____

_____

_____

_____

_____

_____

_____

_____

_____

_____

PURPOSE 7

Purpose is cheering me to my victorious living.

PONDER

Now that you are in the middle of perfecting your purpose-if you have someone around you telling you what you can't do instead of what you can do-reevaluate whether or not this person belongs so close to you in life. I am a firm believer in loving all, but loving all does not mean allowing them in close. Not everybody needs to know the depths of what your purpose is.

PRAYER

God, lead people into my life that will pray for me and cheer me to this next level, so that I can properly and without question, know that I am purposely created for your glory.

"Anxiety weighs down the heart, but a kind word cheers it up."

— Proverbs 12:25 NIV

WHAT IS PURPOSE TELLING YOU?

_____

_____

_____

_____

_____

_____

_____

_____

_____

_____

_____

_____

_____

_____

PURPOSE 8

Purpose is screaming, "Wait!! That's a trap! Go the other way!"

PONDER

Any time it begins to feel like you are not walking in your purpose, you may want to start asking this question, "Am I being self-directed or God-directed?" Sometimes we can get so caught up in the direction we are going that God may have redirected us but we missed it because we started relying on ourselves instead of the Holy Spirit. Remember, His leading is always according to His word, not ours.

PRAYER

God, give me the GPS of the Holy Spirit that as it guides me to my greater Purpose, I listen and turn every corner, switch any lanes. In Jesus name, amen.

"Howbeit when he, the Spirit of truth, is come, he will guide you into all truth: for he shall not speak of himself; but whatsoever he shall hear, that shall he speak: and he will shew you things to come."

— John 16:13 KJV

WHAT IS PURPOSE TELLING YOU?

_____

_____

_____

_____

_____

_____

_____

_____

_____

_____

_____

_____

_____

PURPOSE 9

Purpose sets limits on my friends. No negativity, no conflict and no hidden agendas.

PONDER

Not everyone we desire in our life was meant to be in our life. That's why conflict, trouble and issues come. Sometimes it is just a part of most relationships to make us stronger and move us forward without kindergarten conflict, trouble and issues. However, there are other relationships we have that we desire to keep, but God keeps allowing chaos to happen because if this person stays, structure will never take place. Ask yourself this, "Has this person been an asset or a deficit?"

PRAYER

Holy Spirit, attract everyone that is supposed to help me get to my next level and subtract anyone trying to pull me down to theirs. In Jesus name, amen.

"Behold, how good and how pleasant it is for brethren to dwell together in unity."
— Psalms 133:1 KJV

WHAT IS PURPOSE TELLING YOU?

_____

_____

_____

_____

_____

_____

_____

_____

_____

_____

_____

_____

_____

_____

PURPOSE 10

Purpose is steering my boat to the best fishing spot that will continually feed me.

PONDER

God has made us fishers of men. We all have that purpose. Ask yourself this, "Who have I caught?" Or, tell yourself, "It's time to go fishing." Let's draw others to Christ. Fish are a symbol of abundance and faith. God desires to continually feed you.

PRAYER

God, I thank you for the abundance you have given me. And, as you feed me, allow me to fish and feed others in your word, encouragement, love and kindness. In Jesus name, amen.

"And he saith unto them, follow me, and I will make you fishers of men."
— Matthews 4:19 KJV

"And Jesus said unto them, come ye after me, and I will make you to become fishers of men."
— Mark 1:17 KJV

WHAT IS PURPOSE TELLING YOU?

_____

_____

_____

_____

_____

_____

_____

_____

_____

_____

_____

_____

_____

PURPOSE 11

Purpose is showing me my flaws so I won't let them sabotage my life.

PONDER

We were made flawed creatures but still God said in Psalm 139, we are fearfully and wonderfully made. A lot of times we allow things to keep us from our purpose because we unconsciously don't feel we are good enough, or have the right to have it. Therefore, we will mess up healthy relationships, discredit good advice, ignore warning signs from people who love us, all because the enemy desires for us to sabotage our lives. A lot of times, self-sabotage comes from comparing your life to others. Ask yourself, "Am I self-sabotaging? Do I allow my feelings to dictate my life?"

PRAYER

Father, in the name of Jesus, I pray against the spirit of sabotage, and that its tactics be null and void in my life. I speak against the spirit of comparison. I am in this race with no one. I am running my own race and winning by obedience. We remove the blinders of our flesh so that it does not dictate our future. In Jesus name, amen.

"We don't dare put ourselves in the same class with those who think they are so important. We don't compare ourselves to them. They use themselves to measure themselves, and they judge themselves by what they themselves are. This shows that they know nothing."

— 2 Corinthians 10:12 (ERV)

WHAT IS PURPOSE TELLING YOU?

_____

_____

_____

_____

_____

_____

_____

_____

_____

_____

_____

_____

_____

_____

_____

PURPOSE 12

Purpose is exposing the real people from the false ones. Love them all, but listen to purpose.

PONDER

Sometimes we allow others into our lives who don't help us, but hurt us. Those are the ones who we want to listen to the most. They are not trying to be false with you, it's just that your agenda and what they desire for you don't line up. They give us the falseness of who we are and not the truth of who Christ made us to be. Don't make yourself bigger than God. If you have people in your life that consistently do that or maybe smile in your face but behind your back resent you; love them, but love them right where they are. Don't allow their opinions to invade any part of your life. It could hinder your growth.

PRAYER

Holy Spirit, help me to discern between those who are there to help me and those who are there to help me fail. As I begin to see, lead me totally in the opposite direction of the ones who desire to see me fail. Allow me to cleave to those who are cheering me on to my purpose. In Jesus name, amen.

"But the natural man receiveth not the things of the Spirit of God: for they are foolishness unto him: neither can he know them, because they are spiritually discerned."

— 1 Corinthians 2:14 KJV

WHAT IS PURPOSE TELLING YOU?

_____

_____

_____

_____

_____

_____

_____

_____

_____

_____

_____

_____

_____

PURPOSE 13

Purpose is showing me that my requirements will also have "her" in mind.

PONDER

God and men have requirements of me. Man's requirements of me do not always have the best interest of my purpose in mind. You have to be able to let go of requirements from men if they don't line up with God's.

PRAYER

Father, in the name of Jesus, whatever you are requiring of me, the things that you desire me to do, please allow me to do them knowing that they point towards my purpose.

"Whoever gives heed to instruction prospers and blessed is the one who trusts in the Lord."
— Proverbs 16:20 KJV

WHAT IS PURPOSE TELLING YOU?

_____

_____

_____

_____

_____

_____

_____

_____

_____

_____

_____

_____

_____

PURPOSE 14

Purpose told "me", "Don't forget to take a break and then start back working with 'me'."

PONDER

Jesus, when he was on earth, sometimes went in a boat or to the mountains to get away. Everyone, once in a while, needs a break to think about something other than their purpose. We are not machines; we do not function on man-made energy. God designed a whole day so we could rest. The Sabbath Day. Learn how to clear your mind, pray and spend time with your family to regroup, get re-energized and start all over again.

PRAYER

God, because you have given us the ability to rest in your presence, also allow us to see the obedience of your creation and to rest on The Sabbath Day. In Jesus name, amen.

"for anyone who enters God's rest also rests from their works, just as God did from his."
— Hebrews 4:10 NIV

WHAT IS PURPOSE TELLING YOU?

_____

_____

_____

_____

_____

_____

_____

_____

_____

_____

_____

_____

_____

_____

PURPOSE 15

Purpose leads me into my God given assignment.

PONDER

The assignments we are given in life are all according to our purpose, because God designed the purpose of our assignment. Our purpose is the plan and the motives, that have been placed inside of us. Our assignment works our purpose because it is our mission in life to fulfill the purpose God has laid dormant inside of us. The assignment pulls it out and puts it into action.

PRAYER

As I fulfill my assigned task, designated on this earth, I pray that it completely fulfills my God-given plan for my life. In Jesus name, amen.

"I therefore, the prisoner of the Lord, beseech you that ye walk worthy of the vocation wherewith ye are called with all lowliness and meekness, with longsuffering, forbearing one another in love; Endeavoring to keep the unity of the Spirit in the bond of peace."
— Ephesians 4:1-3 KJV

WHAT IS PURPOSE TELLING YOU?

_____

_____

_____

_____

_____

_____

_____

_____

_____

_____

_____

_____

_____

_____

PURPOSE 16

Purpose sends me a reminder, "Remember, if it causes you to get distracted from what you are assigned to do, it's not me".

PONDER

I talk about distractions a lot because it is the number one reason why people give up, stop believing, stop working and stop walking in their purpose. Distractions are only the things that desire to keep you bound and switch your focus to keep you from completing the task at hand. It is a purpose killer. It lingers. It would like for the mind to consistently wander. The key is to capture thoughts that go against the will of God for your life.

PRAYER

Heavenly Father, release the power to focus quickly and not be easily distracted by things that are not beneficial to your will for my life. In Jesus name, amen.

"Casting down imaginations, and every high thing that exalteth itself against the knowledge of God, and bringing into captivity every thought to the obedience of Christ;" — 2 Corinthians 10:5 KJV

WHAT IS PURPOSE TELLING YOU?

_____

_____

_____

_____

_____

_____

_____

_____

_____

_____

_____

_____

_____

PURPOSE 17

Purpose will keep standards and morals in mind when it shows me the path.

PONDER

Why would God ever bless me to go in a direction that has no morals or standards of the word of God? Ask yourself this, "Would God invite me to embrace worldly ambition?" Anything that will distort your morals and kill your character is not the direction of God. Check every idea, thought, person and plan. It should always line up with God's word.

PRAYER

Holy Spirit, help me to examine any thoughts, plans or ideas that don't line up with the word of God and quickly destroy the root of it. In Jesus name, amen.

"There is no wisdom, no insight, no plan that can succeed against the Lord."

— Proverbs 21:30 NIV

WHAT IS PURPOSE TELLING YOU?

_____

_____

_____

_____

_____

_____

_____

_____

_____

_____

_____

_____

_____

PURPOSE 18

Purpose is chauffeuring me the closer I get to destiny. It is the ultimate GPS for life.

PONDER

Being driven by your purpose is a great thing. It knows the exact path God is leading you down. It will not falter. If God says go left, it should take you left. If God says turn right, it should take you right. Always be led by that plan that God has placed in you. It will never steer you in the wrong direction. The only thing that can do that is you.

PRAYER

God, as you guide me down each street of life, make every turn smooth. Make every paved road be smooth. Allow me to reach my highway with joy. In Jesus name, amen.

"And an highway shall be there, and a way, and it shall be called the way of holiness; the unclean shall not pass over it; but it shall be for those: the wayfaring men, though fools, shall not err therein.

— Isaiah 35:8 KJV

WHAT IS PURPOSE TELLING YOU?

_____

_____

_____

_____

_____

_____

_____

_____

_____

_____

_____

_____

_____

_____

_____

PURPOSE 19

Purpose made itself a broom today, to sweep away the pebbles and dirt that's trying to get in my way.

PONDER

A clear lane is always what is needed for God to continue to allow you to move into your destiny. God has not given anyone else your journey. He removes the dirt, pebbles and leaves that get in your lane to keep your path clear. Rest assured, just because your path may look dirty because of life's pain does not mean you are not walking in your destiny. God will sweep all the dirt away and wash everything clean for clearer vision of His will for you. Don't focus on the dirt, move forward.

PRAYER

God, deliver me from each and everything that I have done. Create in me a clean heart. Remove, far from me, evil thinking and doing. Allow me to walk in pureness. In Jesus name, amen.

"Teach me thy way, O LORD, and lead me in a plain path, because of mine enemies."
— Psalm 27:11 KJV

WHAT IS PURPOSE TELLING YOU?

PURPOSE 20

Purpose held distractions hostage so I could focus on my goals.

PONDER

Life is designed to embrace lessons and reach your goals. In order to reach your goals, learning lessons become paramount in staying humble while achieving your greatness. Ignore anything that will try to distract you and knock you off balance. Balance in life keeps you focused on the task at hand.

PRAYER

Holy Spirit, block out all the things in my life that come to pull me away from my purpose. In Jesus name, amen.

"A false balance is abomination to the Lord: but a just weight is his delight."
— Proverbs 11:1 KJV

"A just weight and balance are the LORD's: all the weights of the bag are his work."
— Proverbs 16:11 KJV

WHAT IS PURPOSE TELLING YOU?

_____

_____

_____

_____

_____

_____

_____

_____

_____

_____

_____

_____

_____

_____

PURPOSE 21

Purpose fed my education, time and ability to move with precision.

PONDER

Ask yourself, "Do I know everything?" (laughing). I am sure the answer is no. No one knows everything. We are all in life's "continuing education" classes. Pick up a book and read it. Fill your head with things that push you into your calling.

PRAYER

Dear Lord, lead, guide and direct my thoughts. Help me to make good use of my time. Teach me how to make the best out of great opportunities. In Jesus name, amen.

"Teach me thy way, O LORD; I will walk in thy truth: unite my heart to fear thy name."
— Psalm 86:11 KJV

"Finally, brethren, whatsoever things are true, whatsoever things are honest, whatsoever things are just, whatsoever things are pure, whatsoever things are lovely, whatsoever things are of good report; if there

things."

— Philippians 4:8 KJV

WHAT IS PURPOSE TELLING YOU?

_____

_____

_____

_____

_____

_____

_____

_____

_____

_____

_____

_____

_____

_____

_____

PURPOSE 22

Purpose caters to my success and alleviates the things that will cause my failure.

PONDER

Stop trying to hang onto the things that no longer serve your purpose. God has all the things you need, to complete your purpose, in your reach.

PRAYER

Father, everything that has come to cause destruction, remove it far from me. I pray against every trap, plot and plan that the enemy has to cause me to fail. I release your angels to go and prepare the way for everything that will cause me to succeed. In Jesus name, amen.

"The Lord bringeth the counsel of the heathen to nought: he maketh the devices of the people of none effect."

— Psalm 33:10 KJV

WHAT IS PURPOSE TELLING YOU?

PURPOSE 23

Purpose keeps me sober with a few failures; with a positive message to get up and try it again.

PONDER

Sometimes we need something to knock us off our high horse to know that just because you succeeded this time, does not mean that you will not have trials, troubles or sometimes failures. Failure keeps you humble. It allows you to see that in every situation you can't leave God. You need God.

PRAYER

God, always keep me with a gracious and humble heart. Knowing that nothing great that happens in my life, happens apart from you. In Jesus name, amen.

"Humble yourselves therefore under the mighty hand of God, that he may exalt you in due time."

— 1 Peter 5:6 KJV

WHAT IS PURPOSE TELLING YOU?

_____

_____

_____

_____

_____

_____

_____

_____

_____

_____

_____

_____

_____

PURPOSE 24

Purpose says, "This person is draining you. I need you to stay watered for the end".

PONDER

Being drained takes away all your energy and you feel dry and unfruitful. Make sure the people that surround you are able to water (revive) you, like you water them.

PRAYER

Heavenly Father, I speak revival in each and every heart and mind. Water all the dry places and allow them to overflow with more growth. In Jesus name, amen.

"The liberal soul shall be made fat: and he that watereth shall be watered also himself."

— Proverbs 11:25 KJV

WHAT IS PURPOSE TELLING YOU?

_____

_____

_____

_____

_____

_____

_____

_____

_____

_____

_____

_____

_____

PURPOSE 25

Purpose draws out what God has put in to bless you.

PONDER

The Bible says in Jeremiah, that before you were formed inside your mother's belly, God already knew who you would become. He put things inside of you that will cause this life to be enjoyable. You have to seek Him and let Him pull those things out of you.

PRAYER

Dear Lord, everything that you have placed in me, help me to use completely. Guide me to pull out every idea, gifting and anointing that will be used only for Your glory. In Jesus name, amen.

"Before I formed thee in the belly I knew thee; and before thou camest forth out of the womb I sanctified thee, and I ordained thee a prophet unto the nations."
— Jeremiah 1:5 KJV

WHAT IS PURPOSE TELLING YOU?

_____

_____

_____

_____

_____

_____

_____

_____

_____

_____

_____

_____

_____

PURPOSE 26

Purpose corrects your wrongs with right ideas.

PONDER

Ask yourself this question, "What ideas that I have tried, have failed? MANY. What ideas that God gave me have failed? NONE." You can have a great idea but not a God-given idea. Ask God for direction with your plans and ideas and you will be successful.

PRAYER

Heavenly Father, in every decision I make, lead, guide and direct me. Help me to discern the difference between my ideas and Yours. Knowing that failure will not happen if you are my driver. In Jesus name, amen.

"Without counsel purposes are disappointed: but in the multitude of counsellors they are established."
                                        — Proverbs 15:22 KJV

(Note: Make sure the multitude has wisdom.)

WHAT IS PURPOSE TELLING YOU?

_____

_____

_____

_____

_____

_____

_____

_____

_____

_____

_____

_____

_____

_____

PURPOSE 27

Purpose changes the way you feel about others. It makes you want everyone to meet your new friend (Purpose).

PONDER

Now that you know how important purpose is, you will begin to desire that everyone discover theirs. We all have one. You will find yourself encouraging others to tap into their purpose.

PRAYER

God, everyone that is connected to me spiritually and naturally, let them find their calling. Help them to accept it, understand it and uncover it so it can bless their lives. In Jesus name, amen.

"But I have prayed for thee, that thy faith fail not: and when thou art converted, strengthen thy brethren."
— Luke 22:32 KJV

WHAT IS PURPOSE TELLING YOU?

_____

_____

_____

_____

_____

_____

_____

_____

_____

_____

_____

_____

_____

PURPOSE 28

Purpose desires for the whole you to be great! Stay the course. Your life is starting to resemble your purpose.

PONDER

When we are in the process of fulfilling our purpose, it opens up the positive in other areas. We work harder on our jobs, we desire more education and we desire to be healthier in our bodies. Purpose has a way of fueling us to improve the total package. Again, these things bring us into alignment. Total balance.

PRAYER

Holy Spirit, as I work on my purpose, empower me to get healthier and more mature in my relationships, and come closer to You. In Jesus name, amen.

"But let patience have its perfect work, that you may be perfect and complete, lacking nothing."
— John 1:4 NIV

WHAT IS PURPOSE TELLING YOU?

_____

_____

_____

_____

_____

_____

_____

_____

_____

_____

_____

_____

_____

PURPOSE 29

Purpose does not discriminate; not even for itself. No one comes before God.

PONDER

Remember, God is the source of everything. Everything you desire in life can be given to you, if you seek God first. He comes before your spouse, children, job and yes also Purpose. He is the Supreme Being and should be revered, loved, honored, celebrated and worshipped as such.

PRAYER

God, I love you above all things. Your name is above every name. You are Almighty! You are the first and the last, the beginning and the end! I love you above all, unconditionally. I decree and declare a closer walk with You. In Jesus name, amen.

"Thou shalt have no other gods before me."
— Exodus 20:3 KJV

WHAT IS PURPOSE TELLING YOU?

_____

_____

_____

_____

_____

_____

_____

_____

_____

_____

_____

_____

_____

PURPOSE 30

Purpose is never out of style. It is on the pulse of fashion for your life.

PONDER

Purpose is always in fashion. It is innovative and always ready for the next new thing. God has designed all of us with something that has not been done before, or hasn't been done our way. Our job is to figure out what our purpose is on the cusp of and make it happen.

PRAYER

Holy Spirit, design our purpose to rock the runway in our lives. Make our high fashion ideas be the designer's original. In Jesus name, amen.

"Therefore, as God's chosen people, holy and dearly loved, clothe yourselves with compassion, kindness, humility, gentleness and patience."

— Colossians 3:12 NIV

WHAT IS PURPOSE TELLING YOU?

_____

_____

_____

_____

_____

_____

_____

_____

_____

_____

_____

_____

_____

PURPOSE 31

Purpose has a way of stepping aside until God transforms your desire to want it.

PONDER

Purpose will find you, but you must also pursue it. It is impossible to perfect your purpose without knowing and understanding God's plan for your life. Pursue it, search it out and embrace and perfect your purpose.

PRAYER

Thank you God, for the revealing of my purpose. Help me to fully immerse myself in the meaning of my purpose.

"And be not conformed to this world: but be ye transformed by the renewing of your mind, that ye may prove what is that good, and acceptable, and perfect, will of God."

— Romans 12:2 NIV

WHAT IS PURPOSE TELLING YOU?

_____

_____

_____

_____

_____

_____

_____

_____

_____

_____

_____

_____

_____